D1716581

COVERT CAREERS
Jobs You Can't Talk About

INSIDE THE
SPECIAL FORCES

LOUISE SPILSBURY

LUCENT
PRESS

Published in 2019 by
Lucent Press, an Imprint of Greenhaven Publishing, LLC
353 3rd Avenue
Suite 255
New York, NY 10010

Produced for Lucent by Calcium
Designers: Paul Myerscough and Jeni Child
Picture researcher: Rachel Blount
Editors: Sarah Eason and Jennifer Sanderson

Picture credits: Cover: Wikimedia Commons: U.S. Navy photo by Senior Chief Mass Communication
Specialist Andrew McKaskle; Inside: Defense Intelligence Agency: National Archives: p. 13; Defense
Logisitics Agency: Staff Sgt. Jason Hull: pp. 16–17t; Shutterstock: Getmilitaryphotos: p. 5; U.S. Air Force:
Senior Airman Ryan Callaghan: p. 18; Senior Airman Ryan Conroy: pp. 14, 15; Tech. Sgt. Steve Elliott:
p. 23; Airman 1st Class Ericka Engblom: p. 4; Airman 1st Class Donald Hudson: pp. 42–43b; Senior
Airman Jensen Stidham: p. 19; U.S. Army: Senior Airman Teresa J.C. Aber: p. 35t; Dave Chace, SWCS
Public Affairs Office: p. 42t; Sgt. 1st Class Brian Hamilton: p. 37; Markus Rauchenberger: p. 36; U.S.
Department of Defense: Air Force photo by Tech. Sgt. Gregory Brook: pp. 3, 24b; U.S. Army photo by Sgt.
1st Class Brian Hamilton: p. 21; Wikimedia Commons: Courtesy Asset: p. 40; Tech. Sgt. Mike Buytas, U.S.
Air Force: p. 33; Ashley Cross/U.S. Army Photo: p. 38; DAN DOANE JR./SIPA PRESS/NIST: p. 30; Edited
by Jjron: p. 32; Lt. Robert Fields: p. 6; SSG Bertha A. Flores: p. 31; Sgt. Russell Gilchrest: p. 26; Claire
Heininger, U.S. Army: p. 27; SSG. Russell Lee Klika/Photojournalist SWCS PAO/U.S. Army: pp. 39, 41; Sgt.
1st Class Alejandro Licea: p. 20; SrA Colville McFee: pp. 24–25t; Spc. Connor Mendez: p. 11; Amy Perry,
Fort Lee Public Affairs: pp. 34–35b; U.S. Air Force photo by Airman Matthew R. Loken: p. 22; U.S. Air
Force/Staff Sgt. Brian Schlumbohm: p. 28; United States Army: pp. 7, 9; U.S. Army photo by Staff Sgt. Alex
Manne: p. 16b; US Army Africa/U.S. Army Photo by Sgt. Terysa M. King: p. 12; USASOC News Service:
p. 29; U.S. Navy photo by Mass Communication Specialist 3rd Class Adam Henderson: pp. 44–45t;
U.S. Navy photo by Chief Photographer's Mate Eric J. Tilford: p. 10; US-Verteidigungsministerium: p. 8.

Cataloging-in-Publication Data

Names: Spilsbury, Louise.
Title: Inside the Special Forces / Louise Spilsbury.
Description: New York : Lucent Press, 2019. | Series: Covert careers: jobs you can't talk about |
Includes glossary and index.
Identifiers: ISBN 9781534566385 (pbk.) | ISBN 9781534566392 (library bound) |
ISBN 9781534566408 (ebook)
Subjects: LCSH: Special forces (Military science)--Juvenile literature.
Classification: LCC UA34.S64 S65 2019 | DDC 356'.160973--dc23

Printed in the United States of America

CPSIA compliance information: Batch BW19KL: For further information, contact Greenhaven
Publishing, LLC, New York, New York, at 1-844-317-7404.

Please visit our website, www.greenhavenpublishing.com. For a free color catalog of all our
high-quality books, call toll free 1-844-317-7404 or fax 1-844-317-7405.

CONTENTS

WHAT ARE THE SPECIAL FORCES?

The U.S. Army Special Forces are one of the most elite fighting organizations in the world. They carry out secret missions in countries across the globe, working in small, highly trained and skilled teams. Special Forces units are usually the first on the ground or already in position at a crisis location. They are the first line of defense of the United States.

Unconventional Warfare

The Special Forces are "special" because their main job is unconventional warfare. Conventional warfare is the traditional way of fighting war, in which opposing sides use weapons to fight each other on a battlefield. Unconventional warfare uses less usual tactics and is carried out by small teams of soldiers. It involves soldiers secretly getting behind enemy lines to help and train local people who are fighting against their government or an occupying power. The Special Forces help local people replace leaders that they do not want in power and those who may threaten U.S. interests.

Special Forces soldiers undergo intensive mission and combat training.

Other Missions

Unconventional warfare is the U.S. Army Special Forces' original and most important mission, but the organization has four other main missions:

Foreign internal defense: training military police forces in friendly countries in how to fight terrorist activity and protect their citizens from foreign countries that might attack them

Special reconnaissance: carrying out surveillance and intelligence-gathering operations behind enemy lines

Direct action: missions that are designed to be quick and precise, often involving violent offensive strikes, in order to seize, capture, or destroy a target, or rescue people or things from an enemy or hostile place

Counterterrorism: military activities designed to prevent terrorist attacks

Special Forces operate behind enemy lines, avoiding direct detection by the enemy.

Inside the Special Forces

Special Forces soldiers carry out dangerous and daring work. To join the Special Forces, candidates must be very determined. The training is long, difficult, physically exhausting, and requires exceptional endurance and mental skill. Candidates face a harsh selection process that is designed to eliminate less-talented soldiers from those who really stand a chance of joining the Special Forces.

History of the Special Forces

The Special Forces have their roots in the elite World War II soldiers who worked for a U.S. agency called the Office of Strategic Services (OSS). The OSS was formed to collect and analyze information that could help the United States win battles. It also carried out secret operations behind enemy lines to help resistance groups in Europe and the Far East. OSS soldiers trained local resistance fighters, teaching them a range of military skills.

After World War II, the OSS closed down. However, high-ranking U.S. Army officers—Colonel Aaron Bank, Colonel Wendell Fertig, and Lieutenant Colonel Russell Volckmann—used their wartime experience to develop a plan for special unconventional warfare units.

Wendell Fertig and Russell Volckmann both fought as guerrillas in the Philippines.

The First Special Forces Unit

In 1952, Aaron Bank was made Commander of a special group of army soldiers that started training to carry out secret missions. The group's missions included infiltrating enemy camps, destroying enemy supplies, and creating diversions. This group became the Special Forces, and it was made up of the best troops in the U.S. Army.

A Growing Force

The Special Forces were based at Fort Bragg, North Carolina. By the end of 1952, the first Special Forces troops to operate behind enemy lines had been on missions to Korea. In 1958, it was decided that splitting the soldiers into detachments, or units, of about 12 men would be most efficient. This allowed each unit to operate, if necessary, in two six-person teams. In 1961, President John F. Kennedy visited Fort Bragg. He had an interest in counterinsurgency and realized that the Special Forces units would be ideal for carrying out such missions. With Kennedy's support, the Special Forces began to set up new operations bases around the United States and elsewhere around the world.

President John F. Kennedy called the green beret a symbol of excellence, a badge of courage, and a mark of distinction in the fight for freedom.

The Origin of the Green Beret

President Kennedy supported Special Forces teams in their belief that, since they were entrusted with a special mission, they should wear something to set them apart from other U.S. Army forces. Special Forces had been wearing green berets unofficially, but after President Kennedy visited Fort Bragg, he helped to make green berets the official headgear of all Special Forces troops.

increasingly rare. Unconventional warfare is best tackled by Special Forces units that can gradually sideline and defeat those who pose a threat to the United States and its citizens.

The Special Forces Crest

Special Forces troops are specially selected and trained for their difficult duties. The Special Forces crest that they wear is designed to reflect both their history and their missions:

The crossed arrows were first used in 1890 on uniform badges of the U.S. Army Indian Scouts, who served in the American West from 1860 to 1939. In 1942, during World War II, a joint U.S.-Canadian special operations unit was set up to carry out missions behind enemy lines. Members of this First Special Service Force chose to wear the historic crossed arrows as their symbol.

The intersecting dagger represents the V-42 dagger that is issued to each member of the Special Forces when they are accepted into a unit.

The scroll wrapped around the edge contains the Special Forces motto: "*De Oppresso Liber*," which is translated from Latin as "To Free the Oppressed."

The crest of the Special Forces is worn by its soldiers with great pride.

Inside the Special Forces

As well as being called the Green Berets, Special Forces soldiers are also known as the "Quiet Professionals." They work in the background, often in secret and alone. They are often the only U.S. soldiers working in a country and have to make quick, difficult decisions every day in tough situations, with no one to advise them. People who volunteer for this job must be prepared for the challenge of working in a harsh, uncertain, and constantly changing environment.

Special Forces soldiers stand silent during a ceremony to honor President John F. Kennedy for his support of the Green Beret soldiers.

CHAPTER 2

THE SPECIAL FORCES IN ACTION

Special Forces troops are among the best trained and most adaptable in the U.S. Army. They take on a variety of challenging missions, ranging from counterterrorism missions to direct strikes on enemy territory.

Terrorism and Counterterrorism

Terrorism is the use of violence and threat against civilians to bring attention to a political, religious, or ideological cause. Terrorism is not a new tactic, but it has grown from a minor to a major threat around the world. Al-Qaeda and other terrorist groups such as ISIS represent major security challenges to the United States and other countries. Special Forces troops are sent overseas on counterterrorism missions to stop terrorist groups.

Since the 9/11 attacks on the World Trade Center in New York, Special Forces soldiers have worked with local governments and police forces to watch and hunt down terrorists. They have captured a number of members of al-Qaeda, broken up terror cells, and cut off some sources of funding to terrorist organizations.

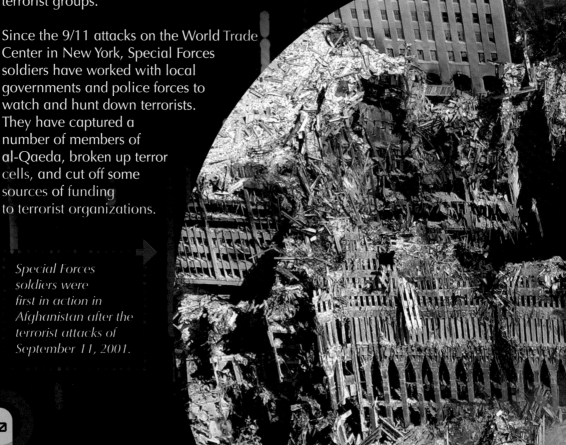

Special Forces soldiers were first in action in Afghanistan after the terrorist attacks of September 11, 2001.

Using Unconventional Warfare

Special Forces units use unconventional warfare to tackle terrorism. They work by, with, and through forces on the ground that are friendly to the United Sates. Special Forces troops enter a country covertly (without being seen) and build relationships with local forces that are working against the ruling military in that country. They train local forces in a variety of tactics, such as how to gather intelligence and how to expand their power. They show them how to sabotage enemy forces, for example, by locating and destroying missiles hidden in a desert.

Special Forces soldiers train counterterrorism units all over the world.

Inside the Special Forces

Unconventional warfare operations can last months or even years. Special Forces troops may be away from home for long periods of time or sent back repeatedly to a place to continue a mission. Soldiers who join the Special Forces must be prepared to miss many family events, such as birthdays and anniversaries, while they are away working.

Foreign Internal Defense

Special Forces use Foreign Internal Defense (FID) to keep the peace and prevent the need for the United States to become involved in a conventional war. FID is a type of unconventional warfare. It involves Special Forces units training people in foreign governments, businesses, police forces, and armies to protect their citizens from attack by other foreign countries. They help nations prevent the spread of ideologies that could threaten a country's way of life. They teach governments how to deal with the growing threat of terrorist groups, for example, by showing them how to keep terror cells from forming. They train countries to deal with people who trade in illegal drugs, especially since drug crimes are often carried out to help fund terrorists. FID units train countries to carry out such operations on their own.

Many Special Forces direct action missions involve raids of an enemy camp.

Direct Action

Direct action missions are short, fast operations in which Special Forces troops use the element of surprise to suddenly enter a country to capture or destroy a target, or recover people or property. For example, they might launch a sudden attack on a set of buildings to rescue a hostage or soldier being kept prisoner by terrorists or an enemy army. Or, they may use direct action to remove a potentially dangerous person who is gaining power and influence in another country. Special Forces soldiers carry out these missions in small units that can operate in a covert way more easily. The idea is for Special Forces troops to get in and out before the enemy has time to react.

Special Service intelligence officers constructed this model of Son Tay Prison Camp from overhead reconnaissance photos.

The Raid at Son Tay

The raid at Son Tay during the Vietnam War in 1970 is one of the most famous Special Forces direct action missions. A team of Special Forces troops attacked a North Vietnamese prisoner of war camp, where 70 U.S. soldiers were believed to be held in harsh conditions. The soldiers had been moved to another prison, but the mission sent an important message to the North Vietnamese: the U.S. Army was coming for its men.

Special Reconnaissance

During special reconnaissance missions, Special Forces soldiers are sent behind enemy lines to run covert fact-finding operations designed to reveal information about the enemy. The idea of these missions is to avoid any direct contact, combat, or detection by the enemy. Special Forces soldiers gather intelligence about an enemy and the enemy's plans or tactics, for example, which direction enemy troops are moving in and where their camps are. Special Forces soldiers may listen in on enemy radio conversations or spy on terror cells to find out what they are planning next. Special reconnaissance units often use high-tech electronic surveillance equipment to eavesdrop on their targets.

Covertly collecting images and other forms of intelligence takes skill, time, and patience.

Mission Preparation

Special Forces reconnaissance troops do a vital job helping other troops prepare for important missions. Special reconnaissance missions generally take place before any movement by the military. The intelligence collected in reconnaissance missions ensures that U.S. soldiers are not caught off guard. Thanks to Special Forces reconnaissance teams, army commanders can prepare a strike against an enemy knowing where the enemy camps are, how much machinery and weapons enemies have, and the location and number of defenses U.S. soldiers will have to break through, such as wire, mines, and other obstacles. Special Forces reconnaissance teams may stay deep behind enemy lines during an operation, so they can track enemy units or help direct air and missile attacks.

Inside the Special Forces

Special Forces soldiers on special reconnaissance missions can be sent anywhere at any time. They often work in remote areas under difficult conditions with poor radio links to headquarters. The risks are often high. If they are spotted and caught by the enemies they are spying on, they could be imprisoned, tortured, or worse. So, these soldiers must be brave, courageous, and able to keep calm during incredibly stressful situations.

During surveillance missions, Special Forces soldiers may have to wear camouflage to avoid detection.

THE SPECIAL FORCES TEAM

Special Forces soldiers rely on being able to act covertly and with stealth in order to complete their missions. As a result, Special Forces teams are generally organized into small, adaptable groups called Operational Detachment Alphas (ODAs), or A-Teams.

ODA Units

A typical ODA unit or detachment contains 12 team members. Each person in the team is trained in a particular specialty, but each member also has training in other specialties. These teams can change according to the type of mission, but usually, an ODA will have: one Detachment Commander and one Detachment Assistant Commander; one Operations Sergeant and one Assistant Operations and Intelligence Sergeant; two Weapons Sergeants; two Communications Sergeants; two Medical Sergeants; and two Engineering Sergeants.

ODAs often parachute into areas under enemy control.

Special ODA teams

Within a Special Forces Group, there are several ODAs that are trained and specialize in a particular set of skills. These skills that are vital for infiltration and exfiltration—getting secretly in and out of areas under enemy control. These special ODA teams include:

Military Free-Fall (MFF) Team: Free-Fall ODAs are trained to high standards in military parachuting.

Combat Diver Teams/SCUBA Teams: Special Forces Combat Diver Teams, SCUBA Teams, and Dive Teams are trained in infiltration and exfiltration techniques that involve both land and water, for example, using small boats that can get near coastlines unseen to drop scuba divers near land.

Mountain Team: Mountain ODAs are trained in mountaineering and cold-weather operations. They also have other skills, such as horseback riding, which are useful in difficult mountain areas unsuited to most vehicles.

Mobility/Mounted Team: Mounted ODAs specialize in the use of ground mobility vehicles, which are ultralight combat vehicles that can be airlifted behind enemy lines from aircraft and that are equipped with weapons.

Special Forces A-Teams

A-Teams are almost unlimited in their capabilities to operate in hostile or enemy areas. They can get behind enemy lines and get out of difficult situations safely by air, land, or sea to successfully accomplish operations. Each A-Team's skill set enables it to operate for as long a period of time as it needs to in remote locations and with little or no outside support.

Detachment Commanders

The Commander is the team leader and is responsible for organizing missions and briefing the ODA on what the mission is and what it hopes to achieve. The Assistant Detachment Commander helps or assists the ODA's Commander and is fully aware of all mission objectives. They are ready to take over command if needed, for example, if the Commander is injured or killed during a mission. If the ODA splits into two teams in order to complete a mission, then the Assistant Commander commands the second team.

Intelligence Sergeants work with US Army officers to brief the rest of the team on information required to complete a mission.

Inside the Special Forces

Being an ODA Commander takes self-discipline, confidence, and intelligence. Commanders have to be physically and mentally fit to perform under pressure. They must be able to make quick decisions and be capable of bearing numerous responsibilities.

Operations and Intelligence Sergeants

Operations and Intelligence Sergeants and Assistant Sergeants are responsible for the overall organization, working, and training of a Special Forces ODA. It is their job to make sure the unit supports the ODA Commander and has all the equipment and supplies needed for the mission. They are in charge of the intelligence needed for the mission. They plan, coordinate, and direct the way the team collects, analyzes, reports on, and shares intelligence. They are responsible for questioning prisoners of war to get intelligence if enemies are captured. They also brief and interview local friendly forces, and they can train, advise, or lead local combat forces.

Communications Sergeants

Special Forces Communications Sergeants keep the unit in touch with its base and different forces. They are trained to be able to operate every kind of communications equipment and technology used in the field. This ranges from old-style Morse code and radios to the latest satellite communications systems. They are also highly skilled in computers and networking. They organize, set up, and operate all of the communications equipment that the unit needs to establish and maintain communications for each mission. They also train other members of the ODA in the use of the equipment.

Communications Sergeants ensure that the ODA has radio contact at all times.

Weapons Sergeants

Special Forces Weapons Sergeants are weapons specialists. They are experts in operating and maintaining a wide range of weapons systems, from pistols to antiaircraft missiles. They use their weapons skills to go behind enemy lines to recruit, train, and equip friendly forces for guerrilla raids. They carry out raids against enemy military targets. They use weapons such as rifles, machine guns, and grenades in infantry operations (fighting the enemy on the ground, not from vehicles). Weapons Sergeants must have up-to-date knowledge of foreign and enemy weapons.

Weapons Sergeants have specialist knowledge of weapons and ammunition.

Medical Sergeants

When ODAs are behind enemy lines in dangerous situations, there is a risk of physical injury, or trauma. Special Forces Medical Sergeants are among the best trauma medical technicians in the world. They are trained in first aid and injury treatment, and they also have a working knowledge of dentistry, animal care, and optometry (eye health). Their job duties include:

- Examining and caring for the other members of their ODA
- Providing medical care and treatment during missions
- Operating a combat laboratory and treating emergency and trauma patients
- Researching and providing medical intelligence, which is information gained from studying foreign systems or environments that could affect the health of military forces, such as public sanitation and water quality
- Providing health checks for local people

Engineering Sergeants

The Engineering Sergeants are those to whom the team turns when the mission requires that something is built or destroyed. They are experts in explosive demolitions and can blow up bridges, buildings, and other structures. They are also skilled at constructing a variety of things, from building schoolhouses, defensive walls, and towers to digging wells. Engineering Sergeants are also able to interpret maps, overlays, photos, and charts, and can carry out demolition raids against enemy military targets, such as bridges, railroads, and fuel depots.

Inside the Special Forces

All of the members of an ODA must be able to work together as a team. While the team is on a mission, each member is putting their life in the hands of their teammates. Unless all members of the team work together, the mission will not be accomplished, and they may not get home.

Each member of a Special Forces team undergoes weapons training.

TECHNIQUES AND TOOLS

Special Forces soldiers use a variety of different technology and tools to help them do their work. These elite soldiers carry out highly challenging missions, so they need the most advanced equipment available.

Helicopters

Special Forces soldiers have several top-notch helicopters at their disposal. The Little Bird is easy to maneuver, so it can get into tight spaces. It can fly close to the ground and avoid detection by enemy air defenses. The MH-47 Chinook is a large helicopter that can transport teams over long distances. It can be refueled in the air. It has a rescue hoist that can be used to rescue people from hard-to-reach areas, such as a mountain range. Black Hawk helicopters are used mainly to transport troops, supplies, and equipment to mission sites. All of these helicopters can carry weapons and have radar to detect enemies.

The MH-47 Chinook helicopter is one of the aircraft used by U.S. Special Forces.

Parachute Systems

When teams have to parachute behind enemy lines, they may have to do so from extreme heights. These jumps are called High-Altitude Low-Opening, or HALO, jumps. On these jumps, troops wear HALO helmets equipped with communication systems, oxygen receivers to provide oxygen when very high in the air, and eye protection. They use an Advance Ram Air Parachute System, which is specially designed for HALO jumps and keeps working in severe cold or heat. The Ram System also has a GPS system for navigation and allows teams to drop from altitudes of between 3,500 feet (1,066 m) and 35,000 feet (10,668 m).

HALO Missions

Jumping from higher up allows teams to infiltrate an area undetected by radar. In the HALO technique, after parachutists jump from a plane, they go into free fall for a period of time. They do not open their parachute until they are as close to the ground as they can be. A parachute open wide is easier to spot than just a single soldier falling through the air, so the HALO technique allows soldiers to get behind enemy lines covertly.

Night Vision Goggles

Night vision goggles allow troops to see enemies and places at night, or in the darkness of a cave, for example, as well as they do during the day. The goggles also help them see when smoke, fog, or sandstorms make it difficult to see during daylight hours. Night vision goggles work by capturing tiny amounts of light or infrared light and enhancing these to make an image. Screens in the goggles produce green pictures because the eyes are more sensitive to green light.

Night vision devices help soldiers carry out operations under the cover of darkness.

Inflatable boats can be used to get secretly in and out of areas under enemy control.

Kayaks and Inflatable Boats

Motorboats can deliver troops more quickly than kayaks, but engines can be very noisy and are likely to alert enemy forces to a team's arrival. Kayaks allow Special Forces soldiers to move silently through rivers and lakes. Special Forces soldiers also use lightweight inflatable boats to carry out amphibious (water to shore) landings, when they launch from a larger boat that stops out at sea, out of sight of the shore. Inflatable boats can also be launched from a helicopter. A Chinook helicopter is able to land on water, open its rear hatch, and allow an interior compartment to flood with water, making it possible for an inflatable boat to drive out of the back. Inflatable boats can also enter a Chinook like this, to make a quick or covert getaway from the water.

Rebreathers

Scuba divers have to take a tank of oxygen underwater with them, so that they have a supply of air to breathe. Each time they breathe, they take a fresh gulp of oxygen from the tank. The rebreather is a simple underwater breathing device that allows people to breathe their own air over and over again. It is much lighter and smaller than a scuba tank, and unlike a scuba tank, it produces few or no bubbles. Rebreathers help Special Forces soldiers swim up rivers and streams without being detected.

Inside the Special Forces

Special Forces soldiers may have to swim long distances, sometimes in cold, challenging conditions. Anyone wanting to join the Special Forces must be a good, confident swimmer and comfortable in all kinds of water.

Satellite Communications

Special Forces soldiers often move on foot and need to have communications equipment they can quickly unpack and set up. They use the latest technology to communicate, whether it is radio, text messages, or through a satellite-linked computer. Satellites relay and strengthen radio signals to create a communication channel between different locations. Satellite communication systems are especially important in remote, mountainous landscapes where radio signals may not work.

Having a lightweight satellite communications (SATCOM) system is vital for covert use on the battlefield and in secret missions.

Weapons

Special Forces soldiers are skilled at using a variety of weapons. For example, the M-4 carbine rifle is lightweight and can be customized with different optics and attachments to improve its effectiveness in different situations. Soldiers use this rifle for a wide variety of small-unit missions. The M9 Pistol is a semiautomatic, double-action pistol that has a rail system, allowing soldiers to attach a small, lightweight Integrated Laser White Light Pointer (ILWLP) to the weapon. The ILWLP provides superbright white light that gives soldiers an advantage in combat operations.

Nett Warrior

When Special Forces soldiers leave their vehicles and are carrying out a mission a long way from a command center, they can use Nett Warrior force-tracking technology. This technology tells soldiers the locations of their teammates and helps them find, identify, target, and destroy enemy fighters more quickly. Nett Warrior is a cell phone-like device with little images that show where people are on the battlefield on a small, digital moving map. It is an invaluable tool when soldiers are in fast-moving firefights with enemy fighters.

Nett Warrior shows soldiers teammates, surrounding hills and other landforms, enemy forces, targets, and the locations of weapons such as bombs.

Inside the Special Forces

Even the most up-to-date technology and tools cannot alter the fact that Special Forces teams are often working alone in dangerous situations. This requires soldiers to have a readiness to accept a challenge and face danger. They must remain calm in stressful situations and also be physically fit.

CHAPTER 5

FAMOUS SPECIAL FORCES CASES

Teams of Special Forces soldiers do important work, and they have been involved in some very famous missions. As well as missions against opposition forces, Special Forces teams also do vital work supporting peacekeeping missions overseas.

Bosnia Peacekeeping Mission

In 1995, the leaders of Bosnia, Serbia, and Croatia signed the Dayton Accords in Paris to end three-and-a-half years of brutal war in the Balkans, in which up to 250,000 people died. At least four out of every five deaths during the war were of civilians. Although the Dayton Accords formally ended the conflict, tensions remained high between the three Balkan neighbors. The North Atlantic Treaty Organization (NATO) international force was charged with the responsibility of enforcing peace. The peacekeeping mission was known as Operation Joint Endeavor.

In 1995, leaders of Bosnia, Serbia, and Croatia signed the Dayton Accords to end three and a half years of war in the Balkans.

Coordination Efforts

A joint special operations task force, led by the Special Forces, served as the command and control headquarters for three NATO-controlled areas. Special Forces teams were the ideal choice to help coordinate different organizations and armies, mainly because Special Forces soldiers are skilled at speaking different languages and have experience training foreign troops. The Special Forces helped NATO commanders communicate with different national units involved in the operation. Special Forces units were posted with each of the non-NATO units and some of the NATO ones to help them interpret orders from headquarters and arrange things such as emergency evacuations when necessary.

Preparing for Peace

To prepare for the Bosnian peacekeeping mission, Special Forces soldiers trained for situations they might expect in a country torn apart by war. For example, many land mines were still in place, so they planned how to arrange for the emergency evacuation of land mine accident victims. Some people in the country did not want the peace accord to succeed, so they had to prepare for how to respond to snipers and how to control angry crowds.

Special Forces soldiers taught local soldiers skills such as first aid.

Peacekeeping Handover

Some of the problems, such as helping refugees and displaced persons, were very difficult. Many such problems of the war persisted for a long time. In December 2004, the European Union Peacekeeping Force (EUFOR) took over NATO's peacekeeping role in the Balkans.

Operation Enduring Freedom

Operation Enduring Freedom (OEF) was the U.S. response to the September 11 attacks on the World Trade Center in New York City and the Pentagon in Washington, D.C. The United States wanted to retaliate quickly against the Taliban, which supported the al-Qaeda terrorists who carried out the 9/11 attacks and sought protection in Afghanistan. U.S. Special Forces teamed up with the Northern Alliance in Afghanistan to break the Taliban's control of the country and bring terrorists to justice.

A fireball erupts as the second hijacked plane crashes into the World Trade Center's South Tower on September 11, 2001. The buildings later collapsed.

In Action in Afghanistan

Special Forces teams worked alongside local forces opposed to the Taliban in a task force known as Task Force Dagger. The plan was to control special operations in northern Afghanistan, bring down the Taliban regime, and rid the country of al-Qaeda fighters. Task Force Dagger worked with local warlords and their armies to capture and imprison Taliban members.

Special reconnaissance missions gathered intelligence that was used to stop terrorist plots and advise other U.S. soldiers who entered the country. They fought the Taliban and drove the organization out of its bases in the north, taking back the capital city of Kabul as well as Kandahar, one of the country's largest cities. By December 2001, the Taliban had been expelled from the cities, and the task force started hunting for terrorists in the mountain valleys of eastern Afghanistan.

Task Force Duties

After the Taliban was removed from power, an elected Afghan government took control of the country, and a Combined Joint Special Operations Task Force-Afghanistan (CJSOTF-A) was set up. As part of this task force, Special Forces soldiers trained and fought with the Afghan National Army, the Afghan police, and security forces, and continued to search for wanted terrorists. In October 2006, the U.S.-led coalition turned over operations in Afghanistan to NATO-ISAF (International Security Assistance Force), with Special Forces teams continuing to form the core of the CJSOTF-A task force.

Inside the Special Forces

A Special Forces soldier must be ready to quickly adapt to any situation. In northern Afghanistan, helicopters were sent home, and Special Forces teams rode through the rugged mountains and into battle on horseback.

A Special Forces soldier returns fire in Kandahar, Afghanistan.

Operation Iraqi Freedom

On March 19, 2003, President George W. Bush announced on live television that Operation Iraqi Freedom had begun. The war was a mission to overthrow the government of Saddam Hussein and prevent it from developing weapons of mass destruction (WMD), which are chemical, biological, or nuclear weapons capable of killing and injuring large numbers of people.

Scud-Hunting

The coalition that invaded Iraq included two Special Forces groups. In the south, some Special Forces soldiers were charged with the mission of "Scud-hunting" to prevent the launch of Iraqi missiles against Israeli coalition forces and Israel. These Special Forces units covered large areas of remote desert, preventing the testing, producing, and operating of Scud missiles. They kept terrorist groups outside the country from getting in to help Saddam Hussein's forces.

Saddam Hussein is pictured here during his trial by an Iraqi court.

The War in Iraq

The Iraq War was known as Operation Iraqi Freedom until September 2010. Saddam Hussein was captured in 2003, and President Bush declared victory from an aircraft carrier off the coast of California. Saddam Hussein was handed over to the new Iraqi government, and was executed in 2006. U.S. troops stayed in the country as some fighting continued. By 2008, eight thousand U.S. troops had been killed in Iraq. The last U.S. combat troops left Iraq in 2010, and the last U.S. peacekeeping troops left Iraq in 2011.

Task Force Viking

In the north, other Special Forces groups, operating as Task Force Viking, worked to prevent Iraqi soldiers from reinforcing Saddam Hussein's army in Baghdad. These Special Forces soldiers trained and supplied the Kurdish forces fighting Saddam Hussein. The Kurds are Islamic people living in parts of eastern Turkey, northern Iraq, western Iran, and eastern Syria. They eventually drove the Iraqi army out of the towns of Mosul and Irbil. Special Forces groups continued to train newly formed Iraqi army and police forces after the fall of Saddam Hussein.

Iraqi soldiers receive training in hand-to-hand combat from a Special Forces soldier in Iraq.

A COVERT CAREER

Members of Special Forces units are the most specialized experts in unconventional warfare in the U.S. Army. Working as a Special Forces soldier is one of the most exciting careers a person can choose. Only a few very special individuals have what it takes to win the right to wear the famous green beret—so, how do they land this covert role?

Basic Requirements

Applicants to the Special Forces should ideally have completed one year of college, although they will not necessarily be disqualified if they have not. However, they must meet the following requirements before they will even be considered for the training process:

The ASVAB is a multiple-choice test designed to pinpoint an applicant's strengths and identify which Military Occupational Specialty (MOS) or Army job would suit them best, if they pass.

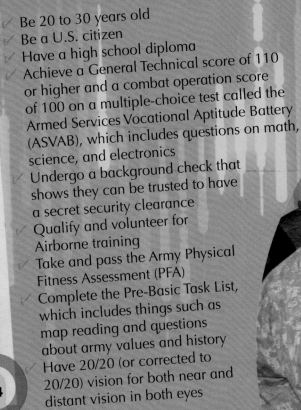

- ✓ Be 20 to 30 years old
- ✓ Be a U.S. citizen
- ✓ Have a high school diploma
- ✓ Achieve a General Technical score of 110 or higher and a combat operation score of 100 on a multiple-choice test called the Armed Services Vocational Aptitude Battery (ASVAB), which includes questions on math, science, and electronics
- ✓ Undergo a background check that shows they can be trusted to have a secret security clearance
- ✓ Qualify and volunteer for Airborne training
- ✓ Take and pass the Army Physical Fitness Assessment (PFA)
- ✓ Complete the Pre-Basic Task List, which includes things such as map reading and questions about army values and history
- ✓ Have 20/20 (or corrected to 20/20) vision for both near and distant vision in both eyes

Applicants to the Special Forces must pass extreme physical and mental tests.

Military Entrance Processing Station

All applicants visit a Military Entrance Processing Station, where military and civilian staff will carry out the interviews and examinations to test if the applicants have the qualifications and standards each branch of the army requires. This is where, for example, applicants will have to do their physical fitness tests and a medical examination to check that they are healthy enough to join the service.

Enlistment

After an applicant succeeds in passing through the tests in the Military Entrance Processing Station, they have a final interview. Their fingerprints are taken so they can be checked by the Federal Bureau of Investigation (FBI) to confirm that they have no links to crime, drugs, or debt. Only then will an applicant be accepted, or enlisted, into an army training program. They take an oath of enlistment in a short ceremony that family members can attend.

Basic Combat and Advanced Training

The first step in training for Special Forces soldiers is the same as for any U.S. Army soldier: Basic Combat Training (BCT). Over ten weeks, recruits learn how to work together as a team and understand what it takes to succeed as a soldier. The training is divided into phases—red, white, and blue. Recruits learn a very different set of skills in each phase.

Phase 1: Red

During the first week, recruits are given haircuts and issued uniforms. Mainly in classrooms, they are taught the fundamentals of soldiering. This includes nuclear, biological, and chemical and land mine defense. Soldiers learn to assemble, disassemble, and care for their weapon. They must learn to keep barracks (where they live) in good order for inspections. Physically, they must be fit, and they run and do daylight marches, carrying their equipment. They undergo physical fitness tests to ensure that they are in their top physical condition. They also learn army ethics, traditions, and the Seven Army Core Values.

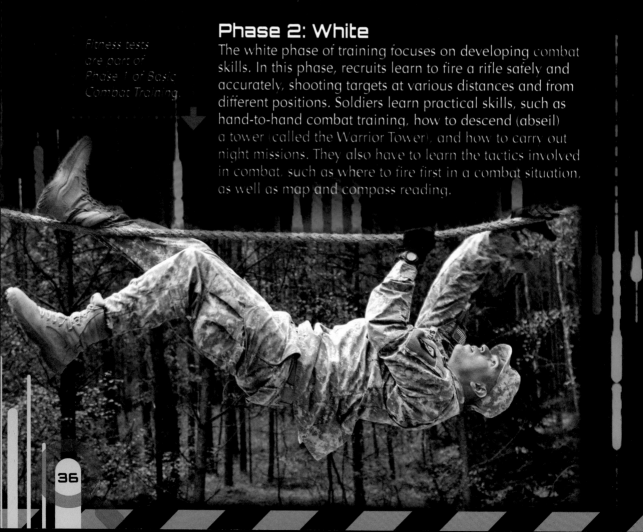

Fitness tests are part of Phase 1 of Basic Combat Training.

Phase 2: White

The white phase of training focuses on developing combat skills. In this phase, recruits learn to fire a rifle safely and accurately, shooting targets at various distances and from different positions. Soldiers learn practical skills, such as hand-to-hand combat training, how to descend (abseil) a tower (called the Warrior Tower), and how to carry out night missions. They also have to learn the tactics involved in combat, such as where to fire first in a combat situation, as well as map and compass reading.

Soldiers in Basic Combat Training pass MREs (Meals, Ready-to-eat) to teammates during a lunch break.

Phase 3: Blue

This phase includes challenges and tests recruits must pass to qualify. Recruits are tested on advanced rifle marksmanship and undergo additional weapons training in machine guns, grenade launchers, and mines. In addition to the Army Physical Fitness Test (APFT), soldiers must complete 6.2-mile (10 km) and 9.3-mile (15 km) foot marches. They also complete field training exercises, where they are expected to show how they can use all their training, such as engaging targets as a team. Finally, they complete the End of Cycle Test (EOCT), which includes 212 tasks.

Inside the Special Forces

There are Seven Army Core Values that all soldiers must learn and follow:

- Loyalty: Be loyal and true to the U.S. Constitution, the Army, and other soldiers.
- Duty: Accept responsibility for your own actions and those entrusted to your care.
- Respect: Treat others with respect at all times.
- Selfless Service: Put the welfare of the nation, the Army, and others before your own.
- Honor: Live up to all the Army values.
- Integrity: Do what is right, legally and morally.
- Courage: Be brave.

Advanced Individual Training

After trainees have completed Basic Training, they start
Advanced Individual Training. Advanced Individual
Training is where trainees learn the skills they need for
their chosen army career. Training takes place at different
Advanced Individual Training schools. The first school that
trainee Special Forces soldiers attend is Airborne School.

*This soldier with
a parachute is
dropped from a
250 foot (76 m)
tower during
Airborne School.*

Airborne School

The three-week course at Airborne School is known as the Basic Airborne
Course. It teaches soldiers the skills needed to parachute from airplanes and
land safely on the ground. Soldiers start off jumping from a 34-foot (10 m)
tower, then gain confidence and learn how to parachute from a 250-foot
(76 m) tower. In the final week, known as Jump Week, soldiers must
successfully complete five jumps at 1,250 feet (380 m) from a C-130 or C-17
aircraft. By the end of the Basic Airborne Course, soldiers are qualified to
use a parachute to drop into battle. The mental and physical training also
helps trainees to develop leadership, self-confidence, and a fighting spirit.

Special Operations Preparation Course

After Airborne School, trainees do the Special Operations Preparation Course (SOPC). This 30-day course prepares soldiers who want to become Green Berets for the Special Forces Assessment and Selection course. It provides a lot of physical fitness training as well as land navigation (finding the way to get places), which is one of the most important skills a Special Forces soldier can possess.

Assessment and Selection

The Special Forces Assessment and Selection (SFAS) course tests trainees' survival skills and puts them through even more intense physical and mental tests. These help Special Forces instructors decide if trainees are suitable to continue training in Special Forces. If they are, they continue on to the Special Forces Qualification Course (SFQC).

These soldiers are undergoing training at the John F. Kennedy Special Warfare Center and School.

John F. Kennedy Special Warfare Center

Almost all Special Forces training takes place at the John F. Kennedy Special Warfare Center and School located at Fort Bragg, North Carolina. Here, soldiers complete 41 unique courses to learn the skills they need to survive and succeed on the battlefield.

Medical Sergeants undergo their training during the Special Forces Qualification Course.

Special Forces Qualification Course

The Special Forces Qualification Course (SFQC) is the final stage in a recruit's training to become a member of the Special Forces. It generally takes 12 to 24 months to complete the different aspects of it.

Special Forces Skills

The first course is a seven-week course in subjects such as land navigation, tactics used in the field by small units, methods of instructing and teaching others, the history of the Special Forces, and a refresher airborne training course. Then, trainees focus on skills such as advanced marksmanship, training in specialized equipment, and live-fire training.

MOS and Collective Training

During Military Occupational Specialties (MOS) training, recruits are trained in their specialty skills, which will be based on their particular background, skills, and interests, such as weapons, engineering, medicine, communications, and intelligence. In collective training, soldiers learn about topics such as the organization of the Special Forces and how they work, unconventional warfare operations, and direct action operations. During this phase, trainees go to the Uwharrie National Forest, North Carolina, for an unconventional warfare exercise. There, they perform as a member of an ODA, and their specialty and common skills are tested and assessed.

Language and SERE Training

The length of time taken for the language training course depends on the difficulty of the language being learned. Language courses vary from a short class in Spanish to more difficult one-year courses in Arabic or Korean. SERE stands for Survival, Evasion, Resistance, and Escape. It teaches recruits how to survive in the wild and use rescue signals. Soldiers learn how to avoid or evade being captured. They also learn how to survive and resist giving information to the enemy if captured, as well as techniques for escaping from dangerous situations.

Soldiers learn combat skills training during the Special Forces Qualification Course.

Inside the Special Forces

Foreign internal defense (training military police forces in foreign countries) is a vital part of Special Forces work. To be able to do that well, Special Forces soldiers must be able to build a good relationship with the people in the country where they are staying. So, as well as being taught to speak foreign languages, trainees have cultural training. This helps them gain an understanding of people and their customs from a variety of cultural backgrounds and nationalities.

Graduation is a proud moment for the newly qualified U.S. Army Special Forces soldiers.

Graduation

Training to become a member of the Special Forces team takes a long time and is very demanding. Before they will be allowed to wear the green beret, trainees have to prove that they are mentally and physically tough, can endure difficult training, and face challenges head-on. Those who make it through the Special Forces Qualification Course with honor will graduate. There is a special ceremony to officially welcome them into the U.S. Army's Special Forces regiment. The ceremony marks the first time each graduate is officially allowed to wear their green beret. Graduates at a ceremony all put on their berets at the same time, in response to an order given by a Command Sergeant Major.

First Assignments

The graduates are finally ready to enter a new and challenging chapter in their lives. Most graduates report immediately to their first assignment with a Special Forces operational unit or detachment. They will finalize arrangements and travel anywhere in the world to start their work. Some graduates go on to take a class that will make them leaders of Special Forces units in the future. All graduates work to achieve the missions of the Special Forces: to train and work with troops from other nations, to build relationships with groups that will support the United States in the future, and to face the nation's enemies.

The Oath of Enlistment

Throughout their entire military career, Special Forces soldiers are expected to keep to the oath they made on the day of their enlistment:

"I, _____, do solemnly swear (or affirm) that I will support and defend the Constitution of the United States against all enemies, foreign and domestic; that I will bear true faith and allegiance to the same; and that I will obey the orders of the President of the United States and the orders of the officers appointed over me, according to regulations and the Uniform Code of Military Justice. So help me God."

As soon as a Special Forces soldier graduates, they are ready to take on their first mission.

A COVERT CAREER IN THE SPECIAL FORCES

Would you like a career in the Special Forces? Following these steps will help set you on your path.

At School

It is good to study hard in all subjects at school to learn a variety of skills. All applicants to the Special Forces must have a high school diploma.

Fitness and Health

Applicants must take and pass the Army Physical Fitness Assessment (PFA). They must have 20/20 (or corrected to 20/20) vision in both near and distant vision for both eyes.

Age and Background

Applicants must be between 20 and 30 years old and a U.S. citizen.

Application Tests

Applicants must achieve a General Technical score of 110 or higher and a combat operation score of 100 on a multiple-choice test called the Armed Services Vocational Aptitude Battery (ASVAB). This test includes questions on math, science, and electronics. They must also take the Pre-Basic Task List, with questions on topics such as map reading and Army values and history.

Background Checks

Everyone who applies to join the Special Forces undergoes a background investigation, including an FBI fingerprint check, to confirm they have no history of taking illegal drugs, no financial trouble or debt, and don't have a police record.

Successful Applicants

Basic Combat Training (BCT): Once an applicant is accepted, they can enlist and take the BCT course. Over ten weeks, recruits learn how to work together as a team and what it takes to succeed as a soldier.

Advanced Individual Training (AIT): After trainees have completed Basic Training, they start AIT. Trainees start to learn the skills they need to pass the Special Forces Assessment and Selection course test, which will allow them to join the Special Forces training program.

Special Forces Qualification Course (SFQC): This is the final stage in a recruit's training to become a member of the Special Forces. It takes from 12 to 24 months. Recruits who pass the SFQC get to graduate, become a member of the Special Forces, and wear the green beret.

First Assignment: Most graduates report immediately to their first assignment with a Special Forces operational unit or detachment.

GLOSSARY

altitude A height above sea level.

background check An investigation into a person's past activities—including checks to find out if they have been involved in any crimes.

carbine A light, automatic rifle.

civilians People not in the armed services or the police force.

coalition The joining together of different groups for a particular purpose or mission.

Constitution The U.S. system of laws that formally states people's rights and duties.

counterinsurgency Organized military activity designed to combat an uprising in a country.

counterterrorism Activities designed to prevent terrorism.

ethics The moral ideas that make us do the right thing.

evacuations The moving of people away from dangerous places to safe ones.

Federal Bureau of Investigation (FBI) A U.S. government agency that deals with security, counterintelligence, and law enforcement.

GPS The acronym for Global Positioning System, a satellite-based navigation system.

guerrillas Members of a small group that take part in irregular fighting, typically against larger regular forces.

ideological Political, cultural, or religious beliefs.

infiltrating Secretly entering or gaining access to an organization or place to get secret information

infrared A type of light that is invisible to the human eye.

intelligence The collection of information concerning a criminal, an enemy, or a possible enemy.

radar A method of finding the position and speed of an object by bouncing a radio wave off it and analyzing the reflected wave.

reconnaissance A mission to obtain valuable information about an enemy.

sabotage The deliberate destruction or damage of something, usually for political or military advantage.

satellite A machine placed in orbit around the earth to collect information or for communication.

security clearance The official permission for someone to see classified information.

snipers People who shoot from a hiding place, especially accurately and at long range.

surveillance Describes close and careful observation of someone or something to gather intelligence.

Taliban A fundamentalist Islamic army that took control of much of Afghanistan from early 1995 and set up an Islamic state.

terror cells Groups of terrorists that work undercover in an area until sent into action.

FOR MORE INFORMATION

BOOKS

Levete, Sarah. *Defend and Protect: Special Forces*. New York, NY: Gareth Stevens, 2016.

Noll, Elizabeth. *Rank It: Special Ops Forces*. Mankato, MN: Black Rabbit Books, 2017.

Slater, Lee. *Special Ops: Green Berets*. Checkerboard, 2016.

Terrell, Brandon. *Military Special Forces in Action: Missions of the U.S. Green Berets*. Troy, MI: Momentum, 2016.

Yomtov, Nell. *Military Mission: Special Ops*. Hopkins, MN: Bellwether Media, 2016.

WEBSITES

This website has all the information you need about joining the Special Forces:
www.goarmy.com/special-forces.html

Read about Army Green Beret training at:
www.military.com/military-fitness/army-special-operations/army-green-beret-training

Read about how the Green Berets work at:
science.howstuffworks.com/green-beret.htm

Discover more about Special Forces history and missions at:
www.specialforcesassociation.org/about/sf-history

Publisher's note to educators and parents:

Our editors have carefully reviewed these websites to ensure that they are suitable for students. Many websites change frequently, however, and we cannot guarantee that a site's future contents will continue to meet our high standards of quality and educational value. Be advised that students should be closely supervised whenever they access the Internet.

INDEX